Coding with Sphero

By Adrienne Matteson

CHERRY LAKE
Publishing

Published in the United States of America by
Cherry Lake Publishing
Ann Arbor, Michigan
www.cherrylakepublishing.com

Series Editor: Kristin Fontichiaro
Photo Credits: All images by Adrienne Matteson

Library of Congress Cataloging-in-Publication Data
Names: Matteson, Adrienne, author.
Title: Coding with Sphero / by Adrienne Matteson.
Description: Ann Arbor, Michigan : Cherry Lake Publishing, [2017] | Series:
    21st Century Skills Innovation Library. Makers as innovators junior |
    Audience: K to grade 3. | Includes bibliographical references and index.
Identifiers: LCCN 2016055218| ISBN 9781634726955 (lib. bdg.) | ISBN
    9781634727280 (pbk.) | ISBN 9781634727617 (pdf) | ISBN 9781634727945
    (ebook)
Subjects: LCSH: Robots—Programming—Juvenile literature. | Computer
    Programming—Juvenile literature.
Classification: LCC TJ211.2 .M37435 2017 | DDC 629.8/932—dc23 LC record available
    at https://lccn.loc.gov/2016055218

Cherry Lake Publishing would like to acknowledge the work of the Partnership for
21st Century Learning. Please visit *www.p21.org* for more information.

Printed in the United States of America
Corporate Graphics

A Note to Adults: Please review the instructions for the activities in this book before allowing children to do them. Be sure to help them with any activities you do not think they can safely complete on their own.

A Note to Kids: Be sure to ask an adult for help with these activities when you need it. Always put your safety first!

Table of Contents

Meet Sphero 5

How Sphero Works 7

Getting Started 9

Go, Sphero, Go! 11

Made for Play 13

A Sensitive Robot 15

MacroLab 17

Lightning Lab 19

Give It a Try! 21

Glossary 22

Find Out More 23

Index 24

About the Author 24

Sphero SPRK+ can be programmed using the Lightning Lab application.

Meet Sphero

Have you ever wanted to own a robot of your very own? Meet Sphero! Sphero is a robotic ball that can be controlled using a tablet or smartphone. Sphero started out as a toy. Now, it is used to teach kids how to write computer programs.

Look at Sphero up close! Use the Robot Reveal screen in the Lightning Lab app to find out what each part is.

How Sphero Works

The outside of Sphero is a hard shell made of very strong plastic. On the inside is a robot that stays upright as the plastic ball around it rolls. It does this using two motors and a **gyroscope**. Also inside the ball are **LED** lights that can change colors.

Choose Robot

Tap a Robot to Connect

Sphero/SPRK   SPRK+   BB-8   Ollie

SPRK+ Connecting...

Sphero connects to your device with Bluetooth. You will know when SPRK+ is connected!

Getting Started

You need a tablet or smartphone to use Sphero. Get started by **pairing** the Sphero with your device. Tap the Sphero to turn it on. Then open the Sphero Go or Lightning Lab app on your device. The app will search for nearby robots. Select your Sphero when it shows up on the screen.

Other Sphero Robots

Ollie: This Sphero is made for racing. Ollie goes 14 miles (22.5 kilometers) per hour!

BB-8: This Sphero looks and moves like the droid from *Star Wars: The Force Awakens.*

When Sphero's bright blue taillight is facing you, it is ready to roll.

Go, Sphero, Go!

Before you can drive your Sphero, you need to adjust its taillight. The taillight is a small blue light on Sphero. It shows where the back side of the robot is. When the light is pointed at you, Sphero is ready to drive.

Use your device screen to control Sphero. Push UP to go forward and DOWN to go backward.

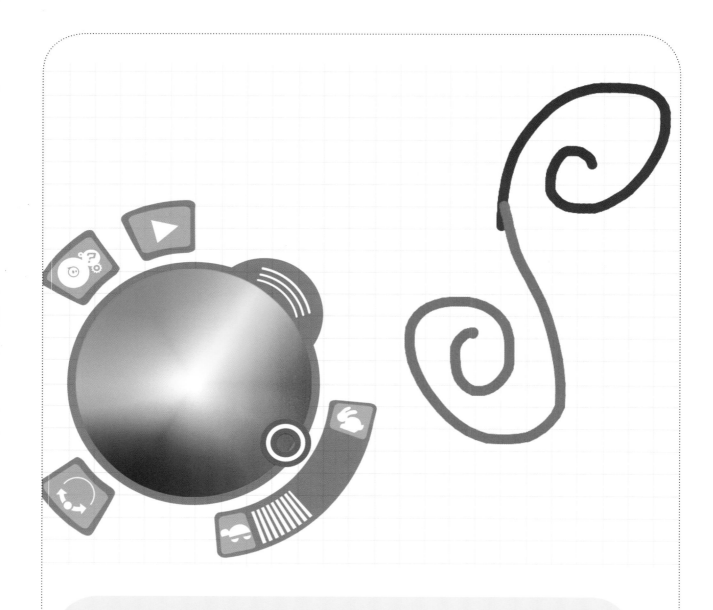

In the Draw N' Drive app, you draw the picture, and Sphero will drive it. Try changing colors or writing your name!

Made for Play

There are a lot of ways you can play with Sphero. Hold it in your hand like a controller for video games such as *Exile*. Drive it into a cup to play Sphero golf. You can even use the Draw N' Drive app to draw a path on your device screen for Sphero to follow.

Sphero can sense when it runs into another object, and even when it is falling.

A Sensitive Robot

A Sphero robot uses **sensors** to keep track of the way it moves. It can tell how fast it is going and in which direction it is moving. It knows if it hits another object or if it is falling through the air. You can use Sphero's sensors to program it to react in different ways.

Sphero's Inventors

Inventors Ian Bernstein and Adam Wilson have always loved making robots. They teamed up in 2010 to create Sphero. They built the robot because they wanted to create something fun to control with their smartphones.

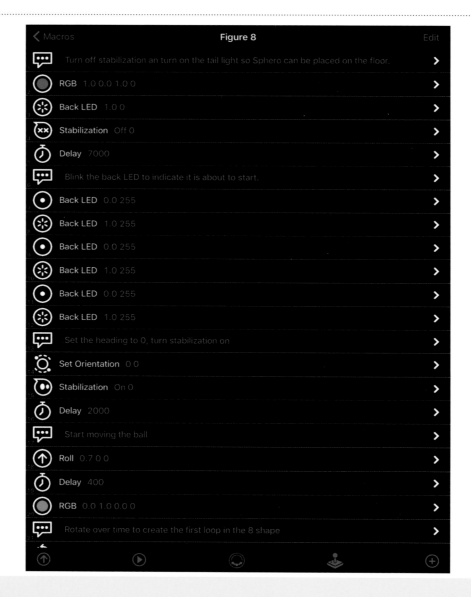

Turn off stabilization an turn on the tail light so Sphero can be placed on the floor.

RGB   1.0 0.0 1.0 0

Back LED   1.0 0

Stabilization   Off 0

Delay   7000

Blink the back LED to indicate it is about to start.

Back LED   0.0 255

Back LED   1.0 255

Back LED   0.0 255

Back LED   1.0 255

Back LED   0.0 255

Back LED   1.0 255

Set the heading to 0, turn stabilization on

Set Orientation   0 0

Stabilization   On 0

Delay   2000

Start moving the ball

Roll   0.7 0 0

Delay   400

RGB   0.0 1.0 0.0 0

Rotate over time to create the first loop in the 8 shape

You can write programs in the MacroLab. This macro, or program, makes Sphero drive in a figure eight.

MacroLab

If you are ready for a challenge, try creating a macro in the MacroLab app. A macro is a simple computer program that tells Sphero what to do. MacroLab uses symbols to represent instructions for Sphero. For example, an arrow tells Sphero to roll. A stop sign tells it to stop.

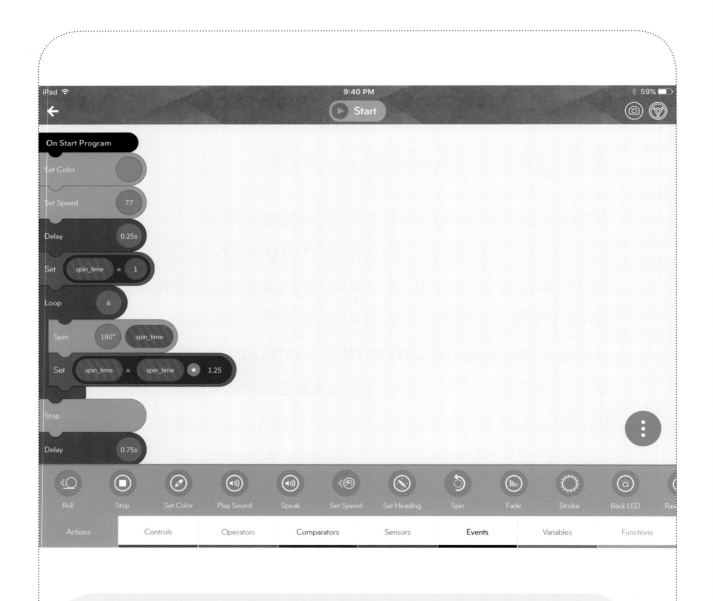

The SPRK Lightning Lab is where you can write programs for Sphero. This is a program for making Sphero spin!

Lightning Lab

Another way to write a program for Sphero is to use the Lightning Lab app. Lightning Lab lets you snap colorful blocks together to create programs. Blocks of different colors have different jobs. Blue-green "action" blocks make changes to Sphero's movements or lights. Purple "control" blocks tell Sphero when to perform an action.

With the right tools, there is no limit to the fun you will have!

Give It a Try!

Time to give it a try! The best way to start programming is to borrow a program that is already made. MacroLab and Lightning Lab both come with sample programs for you to try. Choose one, then try making small changes to see what happens. Every **maker** must be ready to tinker!

Sphero for Makers

Sphero makes a great engine for inventions that can move or spin. Try making Sphero power a car. Sphero can swim, too. Sphero can even paint. There is no limit to what you can do with a creative program.

Glossary

gyroscope (JYE-ruh-skope) a device inside of Sphero and other objects that measures movement and direction

LED (EL EE DEE) a small light that uses very little energy and gives off very little heat; LED stands for "light-emitting diode"

maker (MAY-kur) a creative person who makes everything from artwork and useful objects to robots and computer programs

pairing (PARE-ing) connecting two devices using a wireless communication method such as Bluetooth

sensors (SEN-surz) instruments that can detect and measure changes and transmit the information to a controlling device

Find Out More

Books

Lovett, Amber. *Coding with Blockly*. Ann Arbor, MI: Cherry Lake Publishing, 2017.

Lovett, Amber. *Controlling an Ozobot*. Ann Arbor, MI: Cherry Lake Publishing, 2017.

Matteson, Adrienne. *Coding with ScratchJr*. Ann Arbor, MI: Cherry Lake Publishing, 2017.

Web Sites
Lightning Lab
http://edu.sphero.com
Check out some Sphero project ideas and download sample programs.

Sphero
www.sphero.com
Check out the different Sphero models and watch videos of these robots in action.

Index

"action" blocks, 19

"control" blocks, 19
controls, 5, 11, 15, 19

directions, 15
Draw N' Drive app, 13

engines, 21
Exile game, 13

games, 13
gyroscope, 7

LED lights, 7, 11
Lightning Lab app, 9, 19, 21

MacroLab app, 17, 21
motors, 7

Ollie, 9

pairing, 9
plastic, 7
programming, 15, 17, 19, 21

sensors, 15
smartphones, 5, 9, 11, 15
speeds, 9, 15
Sphero Go app, 9

tablets, 5, 9, 11
taillight, 11

About the Author

Adrienne Matteson is a school librarian. She spends most of her days playing with robots and helping her students write programs about unicorns.